ENCOUNTER BROADSIDES

In the late eighteenth century, pamphlets like the one you hold in your hands electrified the colonies and helped to forge American democracy as we know it. These small books were read aloud in taverns, churches, and squares across the colonies, where they made the case for independence and informed the roiling debates over issues threatening the new nation. Encounter Broadsides seek to revive the pamphleteer's sense of urgency and rhetorical skill to provide ammunition for intelligent debate on the urgent questions of our time. Encounter Broadsides make the case for ordered liberty and democratic capitalism at a time when they are under siege from a resurgence of collectivist sentiment. Read them in a sitting and come away knowing the best we can hope for and the worst we must fear.

Countdown to Socialism

CHAPTER ONE

Outside the Swamp

AFTER HIS 2008 ELECTION, Barack Obama promised to transform America. The current Democratic candidate for president, Obama's former vice president Joe Biden, is promising the same.

"We're going to beat Donald Trump," Biden tweeted this spring as rioters razed and looted American cities. "And when we do, we won't just rebuild this nation – we'll transform it."

When the Democrats say they're going to transform America, we should take them at their word. That's how high the stakes are. We're fighting for our home, our country, America – and our opponents promise they're going to change it fundamentally.

Americans know what's at stake. I hear their concerns first-hand.

On July 2, 2020, I was stuck in Washington, D.C., dealing with the fallout from the Democrats' latest addition to their Russia collusion hoax – it began with a *New York Times* story purporting that President Trump had been briefed and failed to act on intelligence showing that the Russians were offering "bounties" to Afghan fighters to kill U.S.

troops. As these things tend to do, the story fell apart quickly, as it emerged that Trump was never briefed on the topic and the Pentagon announced the intelligence had not been corroborated. But that didn't stop the media pile-on as they tried to gin up yet another Trump–Russia "scandal."

I was glad to fly out of D.C. that afternoon. The Democrats had canceled weeks of voting in the House and allowed for "proxy" voting for members who were too afraid of the Coronavirus to come to D.C. and cast votes themselves. Whether votes were occurring or not, the Capitol was like a grim ghost town. During the few weeks when votes were called, it always felt good to leave for my home in California's San Joaquin Valley, an amazing agricultural region that I call "the breadbasket of the solar system" because it grows more than three hundred different crops.

Due to a flight delay, I spent the night of July 2 in Dallas, so I went to a restaurant for dinner. Several strangers came up to me. They all asked me variations of the same question: is our country going to be okay?

I got the same question repeatedly the next day, when my family and I began the Fourth of July holiday with dinner in an RV park in Central California. It was a patriotic group there, with scores of American flags and Trump flags flying from their vehicles. But the uneasiness was obvious. They, too, wanted to know if America as we know it is going to endure.

Americans already see the nature of our current struggle. I wrote *Countdown to Socialism* as a roadmap to ready us for what lies ahead. In it I document the destructive events of the last four years and the dark forces driving them, leading to this defining moment in our history. The book looks at the political arena as well as the media and social media environments where much of our fight is unfolding. I pay special attention to the Russia collusion conspiracy theory, which has done enormous damage to American society, our governing institutions, and to so many individuals.

Perhaps more important, the collusion hoax, perpetuated by the media, government officials, and political operatives, has become the model for a series of information operations – from the Kavanaugh nomination to the phony impeachment process – that target not only the president and his supporters but also the liberties and legacy of the American way of life. The purpose of this book is to warn of the dangers that face us and to define in detail the nature of the fight and our opponents.

At a time when socialist radicals are rioting, attacking the police, and tearing down statues of America's founders across the country, it's not unreasonable to ask if the America we know will survive. Violence is plaguing the streets of many of our cities, and local authorities seem either helpless or outright supportive of the chaos.

These spasms of revolutionary destruction are typical of socialist movements. They view any nation's past as a continuous story of oppression that only ends with the socialists' seizure of power. So-called "liberation," then, is synonymous with total destruction of the past. In Mao's Cultural Revolution, the radicals sought to eliminate the "four olds": old customs, culture, habits, and ideas. Obviously, if you successfully eliminate those, there's nothing left of the previous way of life. In Cambodia, the Khmer Rouge launched a similar attempt to introduce so-called "year zero," when history would begin from scratch under the socialist regime.

America, a free nation with the most advanced and successful economy in world history, seems like an unlikely place for this kind of total warfare against a country's own past. But in recent years, the Left has wholly rejected the fundamental principles that bound Americans together and allowed us to work out our differences democratically and peacefully. They now reject free speech, a fair voting system, private property, and the rule of law. They don't dare yet admit it publicly, but as you'll see in this book, their policies and rhetoric are incompatible with any of these principles as we understand them today.

As Chairman and then Ranking Member of the House Intelligence Committee, I saw this first-hand as I fought to expose the Russia collusion hoax. There is a long-standing, bipartisan understanding that the intelligence agencies should be non-partisan and non-political. The politicization of intelligence agencies always leads to disaster. It's a hallmark of banana republics and authoritarian regimes that politicized intelligence leaders spy on political opponents and then try to orchestrate their arrest or dismissal from office.

And that's exactly what happened with the Russia collusion hoax – politicized elements of the Intelligence Community targeted their political opponents, used false information to propel investigations and get spying warrants, and leaked a flood of bogus "evidence," all designed to drive President Trump and his team from office. Although many Democrats in Congress may have believed the conspiracy theory at first, at some point it became clear to all of them that this was a gross abuse of our national security apparatus. Yet instead of condemning this abuse as antithetical to a democratic republic, the only misgivings I hear from Democrats is regret that the plot to oust Trump failed.

With what will the Left replace America? Socialism and one-party rule under the leftists now masquerading as Democrats.

With their Green New Deal and Medicare for All proposals, the Democrats are vowing to engineer a massive, fundamental expansion of the government's role in the economy. These two programs alone, if implemented, would be giant steps toward socializing the economy, constricting the private sector and the free exchange of goods and services, and placing vast new powers in the hands of central government bosses and the permanent bureaucracy.

Simultaneously, the Left is working hard to skew the playing field so that once they gain untrammeled power – which they hope to do through the 2020 elections – it will be permanent. At both the state and national levels, they are working hard to fundamentally change the voting system by abolishing the Electoral College, greatly expanding mail-in voting, enfranchising felons, legalizing vote harvesting, lowering the voting age, and allowing current non-citizens to vote through mass amnesties and other means. All these proposals have one thing in common: they will increase the Democrats' vote count.

Meanwhile, the Democrats know they can rely on 90 percent of the media to protect and defend them. In the Trump era, the mainstream media is operating like the Democratic Party's *Pravda*, the Soviet newspaper that "reported" on the Communist Party's infallible righteousness. The Russia collusion hoax, the Coronavirus, the riots – the media's coverage of every major story of the Trump presidency is filtered through the prism of their loathing for this president and conservatives in general.

For example, in a major effort to destroy the foundations of America, the *New York Times* published the "1619 Project." Already adopted as part of the curriculum in numerous American schools, the project falsely ties the founding of America to slavery and maliciously twists our fundamental American ideas about liberty into racism.

This horribly biased information environment is amplified by the big tech companies.

Twitter, Facebook, and Google are all left-wing companies that actively suppress conservative news sources and opinion. Many of these companies have special exemptions from defamation, slander, and other types of lawsuits on the basis of their being neutral platforms for speech. But time and again they've shown an irresistible urge to corrupt the debate by shadow banning, limiting, or outright banning conservative speech for the benefit of Democrats.

Meanwhile, their platforms provide a venue for the Left to make an example of their political opponents, as swarms of activists and their fake bot accounts attack and humiliate people and insist they be fired from their jobs – both well-known personalities and everyday Americans – if they express opinions that contradict leftist ideology.

The Democratic Party itself is now dismissing basic law and order and rejecting American history wholesale. They excuse Antifa and rioting extremists who attack police officers and everyday citizens; they condemn our nation's founders; they are silent as our statues are torn down; and they even denounce iconic Mount Rushmore as a monument to white supremacy.

In my hometown in California's San Joaquin Valley, Democratic Governor Gavin Newsom's punitive response to the virus is creating an underground economy. Forced by extended, drastic, and counterproductive economic shutdowns to choose between obeying the law and feeding their kids, family businesses are covering the windows of their workplaces and conducting business secretly. It's something I'd have expected to see in totalitarian states like the Soviet Union, not in America, much less in my own hometown.

That is why the 2020 election will be the most consequential election of our lifetime. This will not be a choice between two slightly different options for tax policy or government spending. The choice is between two fundamentally opposing visions of this country's history and its future.

Joe Biden laid out his vision in his Fourth of July speech. Focusing on the "systemic racism" practiced by Americans for "more than two hundred years," Biden denounced the racism of Thomas Jefferson and the sexism of the Declaration of Independence. "American history is no fairy tale," he lectured, as he recounted acts of injustice throughout American history. In a surprising and abrupt change of tone, he ended his dark, depressing remarks by suddenly exclaiming, "Happy Fourth."

The Democrats are not hiding their intentions. They sympathize with the rioters and statue-topplers, they're ashamed of their nation and their history, they believe their fellow countrymen are irredeemably racist, and most important, they want to "transform" our nation into something different.

That something, of course, is a socialist country – a governing system with a long track record of failure, despair, and even genocide. It's a mystery what underlies the Democrats' belief that socialism will bring about racial harmony – what socialism excels at creating is economic misery like in Venezuela, fascist-style totalitarianism like in China, and murderous purges like in the Soviet Union.

Socialism requires giving vastly more power to the central government and a corresponding restriction on the people's economic and personal freedom. The only way that transforming a free-enterprise system into a socialist one can improve race relations is if a nation's people themselves are racist but their elected government somehow is not, and the government manages to impose its enlightened views on the people.

It's clear this is what the Democrat leadership and the media want people to believe – America is a racist place filled with racist people with a history comprising little more than racism. If they are empowered in 2020, they will act – forcefully – on those false assumptions, and they will do all they can to ensure that opposing views are smothered and banished from the public square and political life.

The socialists' mania for racism dominates their rhetoric and appeals, but it's an utterly false portrayal of the America in which I was raised. Nearly all the kids in my San Joaquin Valley schools were from Mexican immigrant families, were descendants of Azorean Portuguese like me, or were "Okies" whose families escaped the Dust Bowl in the 1930s and came to California to work as farmhands. There was a sense of solidarity among all us farming families, regardless of where our parents came from. That harmony is exactly what the socialists are trying to negate and destroy. They lump anyone from south of the border into the artificial category of "Latino," falsely insisting they all have a common history, culture, and most important, a common struggle against racist oppression in America. Their individuality and family history are stripped away in order to bring them into the socialist fold.

Socialist regimes tend to excel at propaganda. That's by necessity – socialism is a resentful ideology that exploits and widens class conflict, racial strife, and other social cleavages, pitting countrymen against one another. They have to have an intensive propaganda operation to make this ideology seem appealing. In America today, among the Democratic Party, the mainstream media, and the social media barons and tech oli-garchs, this propaganda network already exists. This book will lay out the network.

President Trump, Republicans, and the lingering non-socialist Democrats in Con-gress are the only thing holding back this socialist tide. The choice could not be clearer. If you believe, as I do, that your neighbors and countrymen are not detestable racists but decent, hard-working, generous, and open-hearted people; if you believe that America is a grand experiment in self-rule that is worth preserving and continuing; if you believe that America has led the world-wide struggle for freedom and stood at the forefront of the battle against totalitarian fas-cism and communism; and if you believe that a million immigrants come to America every year and millions more want to come because they understand America is a land of oppor-tunity and generosity, then on Election Day you must help keep socialist Democrats as far as possible from the levers of power.

And make no mistake, power is what moti-vates the socialists. Their promises to instill racial harmony and to provide unaffordable, undeliverable, free goods and services are a ruse to achieve power, seize control of the economy, and dictate what you can and cannot do in your personal life to a far greater extent than Americans have ever experienced. Practically speaking, there's not much difference between socialism, fascism, communism, and other kinds of totalitarianism. They all share a common goal: total government power over the individual.

The Democrats' socialist fantasies must remain precisely that – mere fantasies. I'm writing this book for the conservatives, independents, and moderate Democrats – the everyday patriots – who can help stem the socialist tide. It's up to you to act on the information in this book however you see fit. But reading this book is, in and of itself, an important step. Unlike what you read in the biggest newspapers or on social media websites, these are my unfiltered words coming directly to you, completely outside the suppression and censorship that occurs in the Disinformation Funnel described in this book.

If you want the unvarnished truth about how your information is being manipulated, turn the page.

CHAPTER TWO

Collusion Delusion

"WHAT IS THIS?"
That was my reaction in December 2016 when I read in the newspapers that the CIA had changed its assessment of the Russian operation to meddle in the 2016 U.S. elections. I was Chairman of the House Intelligence Committee, which had been briefed about the Russian maneuvers. But here was an allegedly brand new assessment – which found that the operation specifically was meant to help Trump win the election – that was not briefed to us but instead leaked directly to the media.

I appealed – repeatedly – to the Intelligence Community to clarify the accuracy of these reports. I was blown off and told we'd receive no more briefings on the topic until after they finished writing their Intelligence Community Assessment – which did, in fact, include the reported assessment about Russian intentions.

The whole thing struck me as absurd. No one thought Trump had a chance to win, and it was ridiculous to assume that Putin believed he could get Trump elected with some shoddy social media ads and low-rent spear-phishing attacks on some email accounts. Some of the Russian ads even attacked Trump. The purpose was clearly to sow division in U.S. society and to preemptively weaken the presumed winner, Hillary Clinton. Yet the media was running a steady drumbeat of stories accusing President-elect Trump and his team of having some kind of secret, nefarious relationship with Putin.

The publication of the Steele dossier in early January 2017 continued this journey into a bizarre alternate reality. The dossier is a collection of intelligence-style reports on Donald Trump and his associates that was compiled by former British spy Christopher Steele for an opposition research group, Fusion GPS, that was paid by the Hillary Clinton Campaign and the Democratic National Committee. Full of preposterous conspiracy theories featuring the President's attorney secretly traveling to Prague to plot with Russian officials, as well as outlandish stories about Trump's sexual proclivities, the dossier was impossible to take seriously. I saw it as a work of comedic fiction, yet the entire Washington press corps was captivated by it.

The dossier was an obvious farce, yet we later learned that it was fed into numerous government agencies, was the source of allegations cited in the scoping memo that established Special Counsel Mueller's investigation, and was cited four times by the FBI to get a warrant to spy on Trump campaign volunteer Carter Page – even though Steele's primary source told the FBI the dossier allegations were based on Steele's exaggeration of hearsay information the source had passed on from others.

And the dossier was just the tip of the iceberg. We also later learned that the lead investigator on the case, Peter Strzok, and his mistress, high-level FBI lawyer Lisa Page, frequently texted about how much they hated Trump and vowed to stop him from becoming president. In the Department of Justice, a top-level career official who is supposed to be non-partisan, Bruce Ohr, continued to feed Steele's allegations to the FBI even after Steele was fired by the FBI for leaking to the press. Ohr's own wife, meanwhile, worked on the dossier project for Fusion GPS, the smear merchants who were paid by the Democrats to concoct the dossier.

What's more, thirty-nine Obama officials, including Vice President Biden and White House Chief of Staff Dennis McDonough, had accessed intelligence reports and suspiciously unmasked the name of Trump's incoming National Security Advisor, Lieutenant General Michael Flynn, the former head of the Defense Intelligence Agency who had clashed with President Obama. And the DOJ Inspector General found the warrant to spy on Carter Page was riddled with irregularities, including the withholding of exculpatory information from the court and even the doctoring of an email to make it appear that Carter Page had not cooperated with an intelligence agency against suspected Russian spies when in fact he had.

The scale of the abuse was astounding. On the Intelligence Committee, we picked up indications of this malfeasance early on and investigated it deeply. Obstacles were thrown in our path every step of the way. The DOJ and FBI stonewalled our requests for relevant documents and even our subpoenas. Fusion GPS went to court in a failed attempt to fight our subpoena for their banking records, which revealed that the Democrats had funded the dossier. And the top Democrat on our committee, Adam Schiff, used congressional hearings, media appearances, and every other possible venue to spread a fantastic number of Trump–Russia conspiracy theories.

But in many ways, our biggest opponent was the media. Having transformed into stenographers for the Democrats, reporters for the *Washington Post*, the *New York Times*, and other major outlets spread the Russian collusion hoax with near-daily inventions of some terrible collusion conspiracy. There was an overwhelming barrage of stories about the Trump team's treason, with each report being gleefully re-reported by all the other mainstream outlets and then relentlessly hyped on cable news and the network Sunday shows. Some of the reporters for the biggest outlets wrote entire books on the collusion conspiracy, vesting their personal credibility in these conspiracy theories being real.

Having gone all-in on collusion, the media furiously rejected all the indications of abuses by the FBI and Department of Justice. As the Steele dossier became increasingly discredited, they switched from promoting its claims to denying the dossier's importance to the investigation. Bruce Ohr's bizarre role as a conduit between Steele and the FBI was of no interest to them. When Intelligence Committee Republicans revealed on February 2, 2018, in the so-called "Nunes memo" that the FBI cited bogus information from the Steele dossier to justify spying on Carter Page, the media either denied this happened or dismissed the gross violation of Page's civil rights as irrelevant. They comically denied the Trump team had been spied on at all, with the *New York Times* referring to an undercover government agent run against a Trump associate as "a cloaked investigator," while the *Washington Post* argued, "The FBI didn't use an informant to go after Trump. They used one to protect him." And although the media pose as champions of government transparency, they defended and even encouraged government agencies to block the House Intelligence Committee's attempts to oversee the FBI's Russia collusion investigation.

When Committee Republicans issued our final report on our Russia investigation – which described how the Russians' hacking campaign was executed, Russia's similar operations in other countries, the U.S. government's response, and made specific recommendations for strengthening our nation's defenses against future attacks, the media dismissed it as a whitewash because we found no evidence of Trump–Russia conspiracies.

Unsurprisingly, they championed the Committee Democrats' short counter-report, which focused almost exclusively on propagating the collusion conspiracy theory. The media found no relevance at all in Republicans' reporting that *none* of the dozens of witnesses the Committee interviewed – comprising both Obama and Trump administration officials – provided any evidence of collusion, coordination, or conspiracy between Trump associates and Russians.

A good example of the disconnect between the public media hysteria and what the Committee was learning in private can be seen in the testimony of former Obama Department of Defense official Evelyn Farkas. On MSNBC, she had claimed to have participated in an effort at the end of the Obama administration to spread incriminating information on the Trump–Russia conspiracy because they expected the Trump administration would destroy all this evidence once Trump took office. But in private, she admitted to the Committee that she didn't actually know *anything* about Trump–Russia collusion and had seen no evidence of it.

The constant media hysteria over three years turned the Russia collusion conspiracy into the biggest news story of my lifetime. But in the end, even the partisan witch-hunters on Mueller's team couldn't create proof of a massive conspiracy out of thin air. They knew on the first day of the Special Counsel's operation that there was no evidence of Trump–

Russia collusion despite, at that point, the world's most sophisticated and powerful intelligence agencies having conducted nearly a year-long investigation. So they dragged out the probe for another two years and tried to invent an obstruction case around the imaginary collusion crime – and they still couldn't create a strong enough case to recommend obstruction charges.

Despite its eventual collapse, the collusion hoax left lasting damage. It poisoned the minds of millions of Americans who believed what they were seeing and hearing on the news every day, and as a result, to this day, they still believe Trump colluded with Putin.

From my perspective on the Intelligence Committee, the damage was especially pernicious to our Intelligence Community. Highly specialized agencies that are supposed to defend our national interests were weaponized against their own elected leader. Having decided the American people chose wrongly in the 2016 election, corrupt elements in these agencies took it upon themselves to correct the mistake.

So they ran a years-long information warfare operation against the President. The agencies transformed into sieves leaking classified information to media confederates who unquestioningly spun the information exactly as the leakers told them to. Classified information is secret for a reason, and the flood of leaks did tremendous damage. Allied intelligence agencies have to wonder whether secrets they share with the United States will suddenly appear in newspaper headlines.

Even more important, the operation undermined the faith of millions of Americans in their own government's intelligence services. They understand these agencies are entrusted with awesome powers that are terrifying if aimed against American citizens for political purposes. Their attempt to overthrow Trump was an attack on our civil liberties, our democracy, and our nation as a whole.

The Democrats' contribution to the Russia collusion hoax was shameful. In order to achieve a specifically anti-democratic outcome – the toppling of an elected Republican president – they uniformly betrayed what they had long claimed to be core Democratic values – defending civil liberties and skepticism of the surveillance state. They cheered on leakers of classified information, excused and defended unconscionable violations of Americans' civil rights, labeled entirely innocent American citizens as Russian stooges, put their full trust and faith in unaccountable intelligence officials running a domestic information operation, denounced attempts by Congress to fulfill our mandate to oversee what these officials were doing, and accused the president and his team members of treason based on a lie.

Democrats and the media wantonly accused Republicans of being Putin stooges and of collaborating with the Kremlin. The hysteria birthed a strange neo-McCarthyism, as any Republican who'd ever shaken hands with a Russian was denounced as a traitor,

I've been a Russia hawk for my entire congressional career, and publicly warned in April 2016 that our lack of insight into the Kremlin was our biggest intelligence failure since 9/11. But because I argued that there was no evidence of Trump associates conspiring with Russians, I suddenly found myself being denounced as a Russian asset. MSNBC's John Heilemann claimed anonymous intelligence officials thought I was compromised by the Russians, and he asked Democratic Members of Congress to discuss the possibility that I was a Russian agent. A billboard ad was even placed along the main highway outside of my hometown depicting me in a Russian military uniform.

The targets of this smear campaign went far beyond me. Adam Schiff accused Fox News anchor Tucker Carlson of carrying water for Putin. Nancy Pelosi referred to Senate Majority Leader Mitch McConnell as "Moscow Mitch." Hillary Clinton accused Trump associates of colluding with Russia. Joe Biden claimed Putin carries around President Trump like a puppy.

I've often said that whatever the Left accuses you of, they're doing themselves. The collusion hoax proved that in spades. Adam Schiff, who finds Putin sympathizers and colluders under every bed, has given interviews to the Russian state-owned propaganda network RT. He even colluded with Russians to get naked pictures of Trump – though his intermediaries turned out to be pranksters exploiting his paranoia for a laugh.

In fact, in the entire collusion hoax, the only people who colluded with Russians were the Democrats and their paid operatives. It was the Democrats who paid for the Steele dossier, which manufactured dirt on the Trump campaign ostensibly with information supplied by Russian officials. Inspector General Horowitz revealed that the FBI believed the dossier contained Russian disinformation fed to Steele, meaning Democrats and reporters who spread dossier allegations were actively propagating Russian disinformation. Steele himself, in fact, worked as an unregistered lobbyist for a Russian oligarch. And Fusion GPS, which commissioned the dossier for the Democrats, took money from Russian clients to run a smear campaign against Bill Browder, one of the Kremlin's most effective critics.

I'm deeply concerned about the possibility

of further operations of this sort being launched by the same corrupt intelligence elements against this president or a future one. The problem is that very few of the conspirators have been held accountable. With few examples that these sorts of crimes will be prosecuted to the fullest extent of the law, a feeling has spread that perpetrators can get away with these abuses with impunity. This is the most frequent concern I hear from Americans about the entire Russia collusion hoax.

Congress can investigate, collect information, and expose wrongdoing, but we can't prosecute – that's an executive branch function. Attorney General Barr appointed U.S. Attorney John Durham to investigate the Russia collusion operation, and I'm confident they are running a credible investigation that will finally impose accountability. Our intelligence agencies have to remain divorced from politics and focus exclusively on defending the nation from foreign, terrorist, and criminal threats to the American people. Just a few years ago, I wouldn't have thought that would ever be a controversial or even a debatable argument.

We cannot tolerate anonymous, unaccountable intelligence officials acting as the overseers of American democracy, decreeing who are acceptable and non-acceptable leaders. That the media and the Democratic Party acted as cheerleaders for this "deep state" is all the evidence you need that neither institution can be trusted.

I call these media operations "narrative bombs" – highly publicized but false stories widely reported throughout the media, all geared toward creating a political effect. The Russia hoax was easily the biggest narrative bomb of all time, one that was created out of whole cloth in an attempt to undo Trump's victory in the 2016 elections. Now, let's take a closer look at how the media manufactures these bombs and who they cooperate with to ensure their operation is effective.

CHAPTER THREE

The Fake News Complex

Aɴʏ Aᴍᴇʀɪᴄᴀɴ who paid close attention to the Russia collusion hoax saw how the media was an active participant in the operation. Instead of simply presenting the facts, reporters at the nation's most prominent newspapers cooperated with nameless intelligence leakers and "Resistance" operatives to manufacture hundreds of false stories designed to convince Americans that Trump and his associates colluded with Russia.

Throughout the entire media complex, the monolithic presentation of this narrative bomb was staggering. Among hundreds of experienced national security reporters, hardly a single one paid any attention to the obvious weaknesses of the whole conspiracy theory. Every new collusion "revelation" from anonymous sources was eagerly re-reported by hundreds of media outlets, while all contrary information – including the clear FBI abuses that House Intelligence Committee Republicans were revealing – was breezily dismissed as biased or insignificant, if it was reported at all.

As I said earlier, this wasn't news reporting,

it was an information warfare operation. And I learned something about how these operations work when I was the target of one myself.

Throughout the 2018 midterm election campaign, I was barraged by hit pieces published by McClatchy, one of America's largest newspaper chains, which operates thirty daily papers. A particularly obnoxious purveyor of the Russia collusion hoax, McClatchy launched a sustained attack on me that spanned across nearly all sections of the company's outlets in my home state of California – news reports insinuated I was corrupt, opinion columnists and editorial boards blasted me for supposedly hiding evidence of Trump–Russia collusion, and even letters sections were dominated by an obviously coordinated campaign against me. The headline for a long profile piece on me asked if I was a "traitor." All these stories had one clear goal – to stop the investigation I was leading into the FBI's and the Democrats' malfeasance in the Russia collusion hoax.

But the media attacks were just one part

of the operation. Left-wing groups seized on the stories as the bases to file reams of ethics complaints against me, then McClatchy would run additional stories on the complaints. In one incident, an operative exploited the California Public Records Act to get the emails of my wife, who is an elementary school teacher, then he gave the emails to a left-wing group, Campaign for Accountability, which cited them in another frivolous ethics complaint against me. Meanwhile, smear artists such as Liz Mair, an anti-Trump political operative, were running operations against me for paying clients while being quoted in McClatchy attack stories on me.

We later learned that McClatchy's most prominent hit pieces on me all had a common source: Fusion GPS – the very smear artists who concocted the Steele dossier. In a 2019 book by Fusion GPS cofounders Glenn Simpson and Peter Fritsch, the pair admitted they planted these stories as part of an operation they ran against me. Apparently they wanted payback for my subpoena, which revealed that the Democrats had paid them for the Steele dossier. We also later learned that Fusion was on the payroll of Campaign for Accountability in 2018, when Campaign for Accountability filed multiple ethics complaints against me.

What McClatchy did was not journalism – it had no connection to journalism whatsoever. They identified a political target – me – and then worked closely with smear artists and left-wing organizations to create a narrative bomb in order to achieve a political outcome – to stop my investigation of the FBI's and the Democrats' Russia collusion operation.

The media, of course, hurl these bombs at a wide range of their opponents beyond me. A few examples:

> The hysterical promotion of baseless allegations that Supreme Court Justice nominee Brett Kavanaugh was a sex abuser and gang rapist.

> The shocking media pile-on against teenager Nicholas Sandmann based on false reports that he harassed an American

Indian activist during demonstrations in Washington, D.C.

> False reports from Trump's Inauguration Day that he'd removed a bust of Martin Luther King, Jr., from the Oval Office.

> The misreporting that Trump had referred to immigrants as "animals," when his comments were directed only at members of the MS-13 street gang.

> The uncritical promotion of actor Jussie Smollett's false claim to have been assaulted by Trump supporters.

This is how the whole mainstream media operates today. Their goal is not to inform readers or bring them crucial information; it's to persuade them to adopt the media's political views – which are the socialist Democrats' views – while rallying those who already support their agenda. As a result, the media increasingly see no point anymore in publishing other viewpoints.

Just look at the *New York Times*, which until recently was widely considered America's most prestigious newspaper. A vehement supporter of the Black Lives Matter movement, the paper ran pieces excusing, downplaying, and even praising violent rioting and looting, which supposedly "shined a spotlight on American racism" and instigated investigations "when traditional appeals have failed." However, when Senator Tom Cotton published a piece in the *Times* calling for the military's deployment to end the rioting, *Times* staffers revolted. Reporters took to Twitter to denounce their own employer for printing Cotton's piece, and more than a thousand *Times* staffers signed a letter protesting the article's publication. Predictably, the *Times* cravenly proclaimed they never should have run the piece and forced the resignation of the editorial page editor.

If you think about the *Times'* actions in terms of traditional journalism, objectivity, and the presentation of diverse views, then it's inexplicable – why would running an op-ed by a U.S. senator spark a company-wide crisis? Even if he advocated something controversial, he was only speaking for himself, not the *Times*. But if you think about this episode in terms of the *New York Times'* main function being to run a huge information warfare operation for socialist Democrats, then it makes sense. The operation involved minimizing or praising the riots, so Cotton's piece harmed the goal that the paper's employees were working toward. For them, running the piece wasn't informing readers; it was an act of self-sabotage.

As media outlets narrow the range of acceptable viewpoints, they find little use for staff members with contrary views. This is crystal clear in the depressing resignation letter written by former *New York Times* editor and columnist Bari Weiss. She's a political centrist, with conservative views on some issues and liberal views on others, and she helped a handful of conservatives get articles published in the *Times*. In her letter, Weiss explained how that was enough to provoke the *Times* staff into bullying her, calling her a Nazi and a racist, and demanding she be fired.

Weiss described a stifling ideological orthodoxy at the *Times*, where contrarians are intimidated into self-censorship.

One would think business realities would impose some discipline on media companies, since regularly insulting and dismissing the majority of Americans who don't support a socialist agenda isn't a great way to attract new readers. But that hasn't happened – the publications just serve up increasingly extreme propaganda to an ever-shrinking pool of like-minded fanatics. Fake news outfits have shown they'll go bankrupt rather than try to regain conservative and moderate readers with more balanced content. In fact, McClatchy filed for bankruptcy on February 13, 2020 – ironically, they filed hours after a court granted me discovery to get information from their private records about their coordination with Fusion GPS and other left-wing entities.

Having abandoned traditional journalistic principles, it's unsurprising that the papers are willing to act as paid shills for authoritarian regimes in order to earn enough money to pay the bills. The *Washington Post*, for example, has accepted millions of dollars from Beijing to publish paid supplements of Chinese Communist Party propaganda called "China Watch." The *Post* and the *New York Times* both also accepted payment to distribute a propaganda insert for, of all things, the Putin regime called "Russia Beyond the Headlines." In short, the media would rather become a megaphone for Chinese Communists and a Russian tyrant than have any meaningful interaction with American conservatives.

The *Post* is also fortunate to have a billionaire backer, Amazon CEO Jeff Bezos, who seems to have invested in the paper for the prestige and power rather than as a money making opportunity. This further reduces the business need for this outlet to broaden its appeal to readers outside its ideological straightjacket.

The end result of the media's dereliction is that conservatives and even moderates are left voiceless. The only exposure millions of Americans get to conservative or centrist ideas and policy solutions is the caricatures that the media presents when they're refuting or ridiculing them. On many issues, if you get your news exclusively from mainstream sources, you would not even be aware that there is a conservative point of view at all. The discussion is so one-sided that, for example, on the Black Lives Matter organization, you'd be totally unaware that the group is a Marxist organization that seeks to abolish the nuclear family and which has granted a seat on the board of directors of its fundraising operation to a domestic revolutionary terrorist and convicted felon, Susan Rosenberg. Nor would you know that the BLM website directs prospective donors to Act Blue, a fundraising mechanism for the Democratic National Committee.

With the proliferation of conservative news outlets, the mainstream media does not enjoy the monopoly it once did. However, their hold on the industry is still overwhelming, encompassing, by my calculation, 90 percent of the media. Alternative viewpoints are out there, but you have to seek them out.

Millions of Americans are casual news consumers – they want to stay informed, but they're busy with work, family, and other matters, and only have a limited amount of time to follow politics. Most of them are perfectly reasonable people who will consider a wide range of views, but they're only being exposed to one viewpoint and they don't have time to consult with conservative media to get the other side of every issue.

I can't stress enough how big an effect this has on the political battles in Washington. Because of the media's constant excusing, downplaying, and skewing of stories, Democrats routinely get away with actions and statements that would instantly end any Republican's career. Consider a few recent examples:

> In the midst of the Coronavirus shutdown, when millions of Americans had lost their jobs, Nancy Pelosi went on TV from her home and cheerfully displayed her huge assortment of high-end ice cream.

- Congresswoman Ilhan Omar called for "dismantling the whole system of oppression" in America.

- Senator Tammy Duckworth said we should "have a national dialogue" on tearing down statues of George Washington.

- Amid a huge surge in violent crime and murder in New York City, Congresswoman Alexandria Ocasio-Cortez characterized the appalling problem as hungry people stealing bread.

- Joe Biden told a black radio host, "If you have a problem figuring out whether you're for me or Trump, then you ain't black."

I've been in Congress long enough to know that no Republican would survive these statements. But when a Democrat says or does something this heartless, offensive, or stupid, a legion of media hacks springs into action to explain why they're not nearly as offensive or cruel as they seem when put in the right "context." An army of "fact checkers" at left-wing think-tanks, socialist propaganda organizations, and media outlets jumps into the fray to decree why any criticism is unwarranted or false. Many mainstream media consumers never even see the criticism itself, just the socialists' rejection of it.

Having withstood one of the more furious media attack operations, I've developed a simple strategy to counter them: no conservative or Republican should talk to any mainstream media outlet. Even when a mainstream reporter contacts my office for comment on some piece of false information, I won't dignify them by denying it. And if they move forward and print a false claim, I sue them.

I'll admit, many Republicans disagree with me on this. The way they see it, even if a story won't be fair to Republicans, it's a question of having at least some small voice in the story or none at all.

But it's a losing battle to try to curry favor with reporters who operate as propagandists for our socialist opponents. There's no difference between talking to the *New York Times* and talking to the writer of some official Democratic Party newsletter. The media's only purpose in communicating with conservatives is ultimately to discredit them – that is the overall project in which they're now engaged.

Our only option is to go around the mainstream media. Elected officials should communicate directly with constituents as much as possible through newsletters, direct mailings, podcasts, and other means. Meanwhile, we should speak exclusively to conservative media, since there really is nothing in the middle anymore. A lot of the "conservative" press isn't even reliably conservative at all, but they still adhere to traditional journalism standards and they generally hold both sides accountable, which is all we can ask for.

We need to do everything possible to support non-mainstream media outlets – grant them interviews, provide frequent comments to them, and give them the scoop when there's a big story. The conservative press only represents around 10 percent of the market, but the other 90 percent of the American population is consuming a terrible, manipulative product.

The media product itself is only one part of the problem. The means of distributing that product present additional challenges of censorship, disinformation, and unfairness, as I'll discuss in the next chapter.

CHAPTER FOUR

The Disinformation Funnel

AMERICA NEEDS a free, diverse press – we need the vital information and debate the media is supposed to provide in order to make decisions about our country. Instead, we have the fake news complex feeding its product directly into our information eco-system. In the last chapter I discussed the manufacturing of fake news. In this one, I'll explain the delivery system for that product – how it's injected into the public sphere via the social media giants, especially Google, YouTube, Twitter, Facebook, and Instagram.

Social media is the central component of the fake news chain. It's the distribution center. Nearly 70 percent of Americans use Facebook, and more than half of all Americans use it as a source for news. Social media takes the radical, anti-American messages developed by socialist activists and disseminates them to the public at large. This process of developing and distributing propaganda is the key to the success of the fake news complex – I call it "the Disinformation Funnel."

The purpose of the Funnel is to filter,

refine, direct, and amplify propaganda ultimately disseminated through laptops, tablets, and smart phones. From there it goes directly into your brain, with the goal of leaving no room for anything besides socialist propaganda.

Interestingly, social media's role in the Funnel was first exposed by none other than Barack Obama. Only two weeks after Trump's 2016 victory, Obama complained to Facebook founder and CEO Mark Zuckerberg, blaming Clinton's loss on the supposed fake news posted on the social media giant. As we know, Trump later turned the phrase "fake news" against his opponents in the press and the Democratic Party politburo. But what was Obama driving at when he warned the tech oligarch about allowing disinformation on his platform?

Obama's warnings had nothing to do with Russian disinformation. Russia spent a negligible sum on Facebook ads compared to the $28 million the 2016 Clinton campaign spent on the same platform. Further, as House Intelligence Committee Republicans showed, most of those Russian-bought Facebook ads were seen *after* the election. Obama wasn't upset about the success of Russian propaganda – he was frustrated with the failure of Democratic Party propaganda.

Remember the context of Obama's statement – it was after a devastating Democratic loss. Obama was simply complaining that Zuckerberg and his company lacked party discipline. Information that should not have gotten out, information that was not harmful to Trump and not helpful to Clinton, had reached the public. Facebook should not have allowed that. It was supposed to be pushing whatever helped Clinton and blocking anything that hurt her. Obama was angry because Facebook had failed to play its nakedly partisan role in the information ecosystem that had served the Democrats so faithfully during his time in office – what former Obama advisor Ben Rhodes called the "echo chamber."

This was the first excuse the Democrats used to explain Trump's victory – fake news and Facebook were to blame. This also marked when the Democrats decided they need to own the entire infrastructure of social media. It wasn't enough that the press and big tech companies were uniformly left-wing. The Democrats needed to ensure the whole industry was locked down. So they pressured Zuckerberg, and the pressure is still on. In a sense, he's a hold out – not because he's a conservative but because he appears to understand that for the digital marketplace of ideas to work, it has to be fair. He's being undermined, however, by his own employees, who view social media as a crucial instrument for re-engineering American society, one that cannot be allowed to go to waste.

This story also shows that conservatives do well with a relatively even playing field in the media. We get our message out and people like it. We have lots to say. But because of the Funnel, and the intervention of prominent left-wing ideologues like Obama, only a small fraction of that reaches American audiences. I estimate that 55 percent of the U.S. public has no exposure whatsoever to conservatives' ideas and proposals. In other words, tens of millions of everyday Americans and their family, friends, and neighbors are enveloped by a poisonous, impenetrable bubble of socialist noise.

Google didn't need to be reprimanded after Clinton's loss – they did their best to try to help her beat Trump. Researcher Robert Epstein estimated that Google's deliberate manipulations of data may have moved as many as 10 million votes into Clinton's column. Google senior employees lamented her loss at a post-election cry-in at Google headquarters in Silicon Valley. Co-founder Sergey Brin told colleagues he was "deeply offended" by Trump's election and compared Trump supporters to communists and fascists, while other executives promised to challenge Trump's agenda through the company's Washington, D.C. offices.

Google dominates all other search engines, controlling 91.54 percent of the market. The next closest is Bing at 2.44 percent. Google handles an estimated 2 trillion searches per year worldwide, 167 billion searches per month, 5.5 billion searches per day, 228 million searches per hour, 3.8 million searches per minute, and 63,000 searches per second. In the time it will take you to read this sentence, Google will field hundreds of thousands of searches.

Republican voters know that social media is stacked against them. Polls show that 75 percent of Republicans are skeptical about the balance of the news presented on social media, and two-thirds of Republican voters believe social media companies create a worse mix of news. And they're right to be worried.

It's hard to escape the tech giants' dominance. How many times have you asked a question, and someone says "just Google it" – which simply leads you further down the Funnel, often to Wikipedia. Unsurprisingly, Wikipedia is extremely hostile to conservatives. Mark Levin, for instance, one of the great conservative intellectuals of the day, was subjected to a multiyear campaign on the website in which left-wing activists posing as disinterested editors continually revised his page to smear him.

I saw first-hand how influential Wikipedia is when Obama-era Pentagon officials copied directly from a Wikipedia entry to justify spending taxpayer dollars. I was investigating this spending with the House Intelligence Committee, but by the time I confronted them about plagiarizing from Wikipedia, the money had already been spent and decisions had already been made. It was a sharp reminder that the Funnel has real world consequences that shape key decisions determining our future, including national security.

The truth is, conservatives and moderates are at a huge disadvantage and have been for some time. The socialist propaganda that has overwhelmed the media is the result of the political indoctrination that's taken place at universities, high schools, and even elementary schools for several decades. This brainwashing of at least two generations of American students has had a terrible effect on the country and its communities, families, and individuals. It's corrupted the minds of many of our most talented young people and polluted the pool of content creators and other information workers – people we used to call journalists.

Hard as it is to believe now, there was a time when journalism was a blue-collar job. You can see it in the old black-and-white movies from the '30s and '40s: reporters came from the same world as the people they wrote about – policemen, firemen, local politicians, etc. That began to change in the 1970s as journalism became one of the professions, though it didn't pay as well as law or medicine. And like most of the professions, it was dominated by liberals.

By the late 1990s, as the balance of power shifted from traditional media journalism to social media, the news industry began to attract a different kind of personality – people who saw media as a way to impose their view of the world on others. They're not regular American liberals, but much further along the political spectrum – they're socialist activists, even though they often reject the socialist label. Nor are they journalists – it's more accurate to describe them as content providers who fill the Funnel with anti-American propaganda and filter and amplify it until it reaches its final destination – you.

Socialist propaganda serves two purposes. First, it aims to isolate you by limiting your access to other perspectives about the state of our nation and our local communities. Second, by cutting you off, it tries to brainwash you into believing that the socialist worldview is normal. It's not. If it were, the anti-American ideologues wouldn't have to work so hard to make sure that's all you hear and see in the news.

The paradox is that in this day and age, we have access to more information than ever before in human history. But the socialist Left has still managed to push propaganda down the throats of regular Americans. The process is very different from the way the Soviet Union controlled information, or the way present-day China does. Those are closed societies run by hard security regimes that censor information and dam the free flow of information to keep human beings enslaved to false ideas.

The system that blocks information from you and your family and friends works on a different principle entirely. Yes, there's censorship, like shadow banning Republicans on Twitter, or even more extreme de-platforming of conservatives. But the more important – because it's the most comprehensive – method they use to block conservative news and opinion is by flooding information zones with fake news and false knowledge.

Their success depends in part on a revolution in publishing. We talk all the time about advances in computer technology, and how a smart phone, for instance, has the same power as super computers from half a century ago. These new technologies have also profoundly impacted how we collect and distribute information. Now every individual with a laptop or a smart phone is a publisher.

Think of the effect the printing press had on civilization – it was a technology that spread knowledge far and wide and leveled out social differences. The same is true with the smart phone – now anyone anywhere in the world can type out a few words on Twitter and instantly reach tens of millions of people. A homemade video on YouTube can reach more viewers than any major television network on its best day.

Unfortunately, it's not the message itself that determines the size of the audience it reaches. Rather, the audience size is dictated by tech company administrators who control the flow of information and decide who sees and hears which videos, posts, and tweets. Radio talk-show host Dennis Prager's educational initiative "Prager University" sued YouTube for violating its First Amendment rights when it flagged some of its videos as "inappropriate." But the court ruled that tech platforms like YouTube aren't bound by the First Amendment.

The internet was supposed to create a digital marketplace of ideas, not banish conservative voices from the virtual town square. So what went wrong?

Remember some of the slogans from the 1990s, such as "information wants to be free?" Tech optimists saw the internet as a technology bringing together people from around the world and across the political spectrum. They'd be able to promote their causes, the thinking went, and the most powerful ideas and most convincing advocates would carry the day.

Now we can see there wasn't enough tech skepticism. Too few were looking at the challenges presented by the rise of the new media. The internet made more information available, and the new computing technologies made it easily accessible. But social media helped consolidate control of that information, creating a near monopoly of information and a new class of tech oligarchs determined to shape the information ecosystem in accordance with their political beliefs – to the detriment of millions of Americans.

Media outlets quickly became dependent on social media as their main content distributor – who wants to pay for subscriptions and carry a physical newspaper when you can access a galaxy of news stories for free right on your phone? The ensuing decline in subscriptions and advertising devastated newspapers' finances. Today the major social media platforms own a virtual monopoly over the advertising market. Facebook, for instance, is worth almost $700 billion – nearly 100 times the $7.21 billion market capitalization of the *New York Times*.

With the traditional press going bankrupt, it became a mere content mill feeding social media distribution centers. And what are they feeding them? As the press became more politicized and less financially secure, they increasingly turned to opposition research firms like Fusion GPS, which conveniently supplies free information that's useful for information warfare operations against Republicans and conservatives. The perverse significance of Fusion's Steele dossier is that it marks the historical moment when the media crossed the line from news collection and distribution to political operations.

Social media is essentially a parasite – which is one of its big advantages. It doesn't have to pay infrastructure and production costs, like paper for newsprint, video and other studio overhead for broadcast media, or even content. It either recycles content created by traditional media brands, which give their content away for free because they have no choice, or it disseminates content created by people like you and me.

Another huge advantage social media has over traditional media is that it has no legal responsibility to provide reliable information.

Tech visionaries and their allies in Congress were concerned that social media platforms wouldn't be able to survive if they were constantly being sued for allowing users to post objectionable content. So when lawmakers passed the Communications Decency Act in 1996, they included Section 230 in order to "promote the continued development of the internet and other interactive computer services and other interactive media." Also known as the Cox-Wyden Amendment, Section 230 stipulated that "no provider or user of an interactive computer service shall be treated as the publisher or speaker of any information provided by another information content provider."

So social media companies were absolved of liability for what appears on their platforms – which also made those platforms ripe for abuse. With no responsibility for ensuring the information they provide is accurate, the tech firms have turned their platforms into syndicates for disseminating socialist propaganda.

Further, as the *Prager University v. You-Tube* case shows, social media wants to have it both ways. When it's convenient, it's not a content provider, so it can't be sued like a publisher can. But when it wants to act like a publisher and shape an editorial message by promoting and spreading one side of the debate while suppressing, de-boosting, and shadow banning the other side, it claims to enjoy impunity from all lawsuits that would impose accountability.

Social media platforms have to be forced to decide: if they want to enjoy continued protection under Section 230 then they should offer, as the law stipulates, "a forum for a true diversity of political discourse." But if they're going to act as political propagandists for one viewpoint and one political party, which is what they're doing now, then

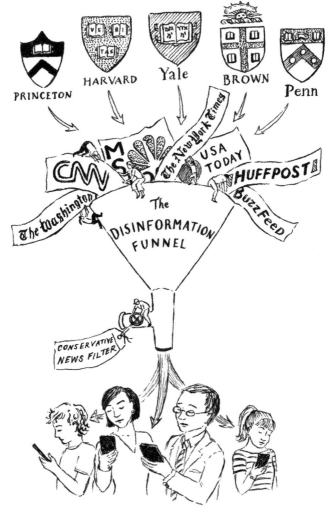

THE DISINFORMATION FUNNEL FLOW

Around 55 percent of the American population is completely cut off from viewpoints and arguments that contradict the socialist narrative. On the opposite page, see how the socialists achieve that dominance.

UNIVERSITY SYSTEM: The academic Left indoctrinates the student body, especially in humanities and the liberal arts departments, where identity politics and socialist ideology dominates research institutions. These academic institutions process and pass on activists to traditional media (the *Washington Post*, the *New York Times*, MSNBC, CNN, BuzzFeed, Huffington Post, etc.) and social media brands (Twitter, Facebook, Google, etc.).

THE MEDIA: Socialist activists at traditional media organizations design content to be passed through social media platforms and distributed to the public. Headline writers play an important part of the process since the headlines are typically used as the basis for social media messaging. The majority of social media users, 60 percent, who pass on a link in a tweet or post do not click through the link to the article. It's fair to say that the social media messaging is more important than the original article, often written, it seems, solely as a basis for the social media.

CONTENT FILTERERS AND AMPLIFIERS: Political activists employed at social media platforms like Google and Facebook filter out information that doesn't conform to socialist ideological preferences. While social media executives claim that its algorithms dictate how stories are ranked and rotated through news feeds, their employees have repeatedly been caught on camera admitting that they regularly suppress conservative news.

DELIVERY MECHANISMS: Every individual with a laptop, tablet, or smart phone can now act as a publisher able to immediately reach large audiences. Those delivery mechanisms are also receivers, connecting users to each other, and to the information distribution centers served by social media platforms.

YOU: This is what the Disinformation Funnel is designed for — to influence you and shape your decision-making about your family, your community, and the country we all share.

legally they should no longer be treated differently from traditional publishers.

As I mentioned earlier, a primary reason why I wrote this book is to completely bypass the Disinformation Funnel to get out my message. This is my unfiltered message to you, and I hope you'll share it with your family and friends. Just like the tech visionaries of the 1990s said, information wants to be free. So do Americans. And to ensure our liberties, we need real news and information, free of the filtering and amplification of the socialist ideologues poisoning our information ecosystem.

CHAPTER FIVE

Information Desert

THE RECENT FATE of my home state of California should serve as a warning sign to all Americans of the power of the Disinformation Funnel to affect public perception and government policy.

As I mentioned, I live in central California's San Joaquin Valley, a lush agricultural region that's home to the most productive land anywhere. We feed a lot of the country, and in fact, a lot of the world.

But due to a lack of water, the region is naturally a desert. It became the breadbasket of the solar system through the construction of the world's most sophisticated irrigation system, comprising pumping stations, aqueducts, pipelines, and storage facilities. This network takes water originating in the snowpack of the Sierra Nevada Mountains, stores it, and transports it widely for use by California's 40 million residents.

For decades, this system has been targeted by radical environmentalists who want to drive farmers away and return the land to its natural, desert condition. This is characteristic of the socialists' environmental extremism, in which the overall goal is to impose population controls.

Citing as a pretext the supposed need to protect a three-inch baitfish called the Delta smelt, environmental organizations filed a succession of lawsuits beginning in the 1990s that forced the state to divert billions of gallons of water away from farmers and families and dump it into the Pacific Ocean. Over the years, the crisis worsened due to environmentalists' opposition to new water storage projects and restrictions on groundwater pumping implemented by former Governor Jerry Brown.

As a result, the San Joaquin Valley is ensnared in a years-long water crisis. Two-hundred-fifty thousand acres of productive land have been idled, and a million acres in total – one-third of the Valley's farmland, an area bigger than the state of Rhode Island – will have to be abandoned if the current trajectory continues. The crisis has created high unemployment in the Valley and a host of other social ills as the livelihoods of tens of thousands of people – many of them farm-workers – have been ripped away.

Beholden to the environmental lobby, Democrats in Congress have blocked passage of countless Republican bills to alleviate the water crisis. President Trump, however, became the first president in decades to take action, ordering reforms to the biological opinions that formed the basis of the environmentalists' most damaging court actions. Issued in early 2020, the new opinions would resolve a big part of the problem and significantly increase the water supply. Shockingly, California's governor, Democrat Gavin Newsom, filed a lawsuit to cancel the opinions that would ease the water crisis in his own state.

The Valley water crisis has spread throughout the state, since many other areas depend on the Sierra Nevada snowpack for their water. Statewide water restrictions have been approved, including limits on personal indoor water use, restrictions on watering lawns and driveways, and even rules on washing cars.

Yet outside the San Joaquin Valley, Californians don't seem particularly upset by the crisis or by their own governor's pitiless determination to ensure it continues. The plight of their fellow Californians in the Valley, the water restrictions, the jeopardy to their own cities' water supply, and the specter of major reductions to their food supply haven't been enough for voters to demand change and impose accountability on their representatives.

How is this possible? Having spent years talking about this issue with Californians from all walks of life, I know the answer: after being relentlessly fed socialist propaganda without any opposing views, many people simply don't know the real causes or consequences of the crisis.

California socialists, and the media that represents them, have a low opinion of farmers. In the media's presentation, farmers are either ignorant cowboys with boots, hats, and guns, or somewhat contradictorily, are rich corporate shills – part of the nefarious "Big Agriculture" conglomerate – who are greedily using up all the state's water. The radical environmentalists, naturally, are noble activists fighting for a selfless cause.

The media often ascribes the overall problem to drought or global warming, neither of which are true. The irrigation system was designed to withstand five years of drought by capturing water in wet years and storing it for use in dry ones. The problem is that the government is preventing us from using the system to full capacity, and it's politically impossible to get new storage projects approved.

The media also darkly warns of various environmental catastrophes if more water is diverted back to human use. What they don't mention is that 80 percent of the water from the Sierra Nevada snowpack is dumped into the Pacific Ocean, but if that number were merely reduced to 75 percent, there would be plenty of water for everyone – farmers, cities, and the environment. The need for drastic water restrictions is being entirely manufactured. There is no actual water shortage – in fact, with proper use of the irrigation system, there is far more water available than we need.

I've spent years going up and down California trying to inform anyone who will listen about the true causes of the water crisis. But it's an uphill battle – it's tough for one person to reach millions of citizens who are bombarded, day in and day out, with disinformation. With a propaganda campaign that's sustained long enough, and supported by enough activists, media figures, and resources, people's minds can be poisoned to the point that they'll willingly go along as their own state is systematically and deliberately deprived of water. If you tell a lie enough times with enough conviction and block out the truth, a lot of people will believe you because they just don't have any other information to challenge the propaganda.

The disinformation campaign is so overwhelming that many Californians don't even realize they really live in a desert. In fact, without Sierra Nevada water, the Los Angeles water supply would reach a critically low level in a few months and San Francisco would encounter the same disaster in less than a month. Yes, you heard that right – socialist activists in L.A. and San Francisco are attacking and constricting the very water supply that sustains their own communities.

* * *

The purpose of this book is to put information in your hands directly. That's what a broadside is for, after all. The golden age of the broadside was the eighteenth century, when it became an important form of popular media, a one-page sheet pasted to a wall or distributed to the public. During the American Revolution, they were used to spread news, recruit troops, announce laws and regulations, celebrate events, and inspire the men and women who founded our country. They were direct, unfiltered messages between authors and their audience.

Probably the most famous broadside in American history is named after John Dunlap, the Philadelphia printer who, on the night of July 4, 1776, published one of the most important documents in world history – the Declaration of Independence. After the Second

Continental Congress ratified the text, it ordered that Dunlap's broadside be distributed to the Continental Army and the thirteen states and to be posted in public areas for citizens of the new republic to read.

And they read:

We hold these truths to be self-evident, that all men are created equal, that they are endowed by their Creator with certain unalienable Rights, that among these are Life, Liberty and the pursuit of Happiness.

That's still news 244 years later.

I ask you to spread the news by sharing the information in this book. It's an example of how Americans can find the news they need to make important decisions about our country, communities, families, and ourselves. Get it directly from sources you trust – blogs, websites, and newspapers – even if you don't always agree with them. There is a group of investigative reporters outside the mainstream media who got the truth out about the Russia collusion operation when the rest of the press was furiously peddling the hoax.

There weren't many of these contrarian reporters, but they reached enough people to have a major political effect. Without them, to be honest, the operation may very well have succeeded in removing the president.

Don't click on what's promoted on social media or what's sent to you on an automated email list – that's not the news, that's the Disinformation Funnel. Although it's not easy to navigate the Internet without Google, to whatever extent you can, avoid using it for researching the news. Whenever possible, use alternatives to the main social media networks. For example, you can join me on Parler, an alternative platform to Twitter, and let's build that up into a viable place where Americans from across the political spectrum can talk freely.

If there's one lesson to take from my broadside, it's to stay out of the Disinformation Funnel – it's powerful and destructive. It can confuse and misinform people even about the most basic facts and most crucial issues related to the place where they live. Those same mechanisms are no doubt playing a large role in the 2020 presidential campaign.

If you'd told me at the beginning of 2020 that violent protestors, often publicly backed by the Democratic Party, would rampage through American cities and destroy statues of our founding fathers and other American heroes, I'd have predicted that support for Trump would be at 60 percent. As I write, in the midst of a relentless media campaign to excuse or champion the rioters and statue topplers while blaming Trump for the problems they cause, he's at 45 percent. That tells me the Funnel is in full effect, and the Democrats know it.

The Funnel explains why the Joe Biden campaign doesn't have a real platform, why the candidate barely leaves his basement, and why his party isn't even planning to hold a real convention. The socialists think they have a winning hand by keeping their candidate underground and messaging through the Funnel. And you've heard the message, it's the same thing they've been saying for four years – Trump is a fascist, all Republicans are racist, and the answer to all our problems is warmed-over socialism that's failed everywhere else in the world. It defies all logic, but that's how powerful the Funnel is. It's convincing people that the societal meltdown engineered by Democrat mayors and governors is all Trump's fault.

Here's what I'm asking – spread the truth. The purpose of the Funnel is to confuse

Americans and subject us to a constant barrage of propaganda and disinformation, injecting it into our brains every time we look at our phones. They want to keep you from seeing the truth and to feel scared and disoriented if you come across it.

You need to understand how the media, the tech giants, and the Democrats are manipulating the information you receive. Once you're aware of that, you'll recognize narrative bombs when you see them. You'll understand the political purpose behind the stories and what their authors and promoters are trying to get you to believe.

The November 2020 elections will be the

most consequential of our lifetime. Millions of Americans will rely exclusively on information gained through the Funnel to inform their vote. Overcoming that handicap will not be easy. I hope this book will help readers take a step toward doing so.

© 2020 by Devin Nunes

Illustrations by Katherine Messenger

First American edition published in 2020 by Encounter Books, an activity of Encounter for Culture and Education, Inc., a nonprofit, tax exempt corporation. Encounter Books website address: www.encounterbooks.com

Manufactured in the United States and printed on acid-free paper. The paper used in this publication meets the minimum requirements of ANSI / NISO Z39.48–1992 (R 1997) (*Permanence of Paper*).

FIRST AMERICAN EDITION

LIBRARY OF CONGRESS CATALOGING-IN-PUBLICATION DATA IS AVAILABLE